D1396024

Journey Six

A collection of images from Travel Photographer of the Year

Travel Photographer of the Year Ltd - The Photographers' Press

Publisher/Editor/Author - Chris Coe
Editor - Karen Coe
Sub Editor - Emma Thomson
Designer - Gabrielle Davies

First published by Travel Photographer of the Year Ltd,
20 Yew Tree Courtyard, Earl Soham, Suffolk IP13 7SG, UK
www.tpoty.com

First edition published in July 2014
ISBN: 978-0-9549396-6-3

Reproduced, printed and bound by Connekt Colour Berkhamstead, HP4 1EH, UK

Front cover photograph: Dongjiang Lake, Hunan, China. **Jino Lee, Malaysia.**

Frontispiece photograph: Tarragona, Catalonia, Spain. **David Oliete, Spain.**

Page 3 photograph: Kurile Lake, Kamchatka, Russia. **Marco Urso, Italy.**

Page 4 photograph: East London, South Africa. **Terry Steeley, UK.**

Page 5 photograph: Ténéré desert, Niger. **Jørgen Johanson, Norway.**

Back cover photograph (top left): Mathura, Uttar Pradesh, India. **Sahil Lodha, India.**

Back cover photograph (middle left): Ipanema beach, Rio de Janeiro, Brazil. **Tony Burns, UK.**

Back cover photograph (bottom left):
Jigokudani Yaen Koen, Yamanouchi, Nagano Prefecture, Japan. **Jasper Doest, Netherlands.**

Back cover photograph (middle right): Phuket, Thailand. **Justin Mott, USA.**

CONTENTS

Introduction	4
Travel Photographer of the Year *The Cutty Sark Award*	6
Young Travel Photographer of the Year	12
Vanishing and Emerging Cultures	22
Monochromal	32
Wild Stories	40
One Shot - Extraordinary	52
New Talent - Metropolis	62
First Shot - En Route	70
Best Single Image in a Portfolio	74
Judges	89
Sponsors and Partners	90
Index of Photographers	95

In an ever shrinking world it is both heart-warming and exciting to know that there are still so many great journeys and experiences to be had. Journey Six is the latest in the Travel Photographer of the Year portfolio series and, after five previous journeys, you can be forgiven for wondering if you've seen it all before. Turning these pages will quickly bring the realisation that you haven't and that one of the best things about travel is that there are always new journeys and new photographs to make.

Looking back there have been so many fabulous images, and each year we wait with bated breath to see the latest ones. And each year they don't disappoint, and the collections just seem to get better and better, with this latest book bearing testament to that.

For many of today's older photographers, photography began with the black and white (B&W) image simply because B&W film and processing were cheaper, and this made photography more accessible to more people. The supreme irony is that great B&W photography is arguably harder to achieve as there is nowhere to hide poor composition without the distractions of colour. But the B&W image has never really gone away and its rich heritage is inspiring new generations of photographers.

As TPOTY entered its second decade, in 2013, the awards included a B&W only portfolio category for the first time. Journey Six contains a section of the best entries, with the cover image taken from the winning Monochromal portfolio. Interestingly, and coincidentally, the winning portfolios by the latest Travel Photographer of the Year, Timothy Allen, are also B&W images even though only one of these portfolios was entered in the Monochromal category. This sixth collection of images shouts that B&W travel photography is very much alive and kicking!

With the digital revolution in photography now moving into history, with the technology of the digital image now established and the incremental advances less pronounced, it is interesting to see photography and photographers returning to creativity rather than being overly focused on the technology of cameras and computers. Shutter speeds and f-stops never went away but for many photographers their discovery or rediscovery is a revelation which is transforming their photography and inspiring creativity.

Travel photography is often accused of looking back and reflecting a world of poor people trapped in their traditional ways of life. This view says more about the accuser's vision of our world than it does about the travel photographer. Any frequent traveller can see with their own eyes how modern transport and mobile communications are transforming our planet. This transformation is rapid and has both positives and negatives associated with it. On the one hand it is easier to communicate and travel, both within and across borders. On the other, traditions held for many centuries, and which form the routes of many cultural identities, are being diluted and in some cases lost completely. It's as if we are moving towards one homogenous mass of humanity, as transport and communications shrink our planet, and the lines which distinguish different cultures, marking them as unique, are becoming ever more blurred.

The travel photography genre started as a means to document the lives of cultures differing from our own but it has evolved into a creative medium for capturing change, beauty, difference, similarity and also the less palatable side of the travel experience. It is not just about recording the past and those fragments of ancient cultures, valuable as they are, but also about capturing the emergence of new ways of life, new cultural groups and the evolution from one to the other. It's a window on a fast changing world.

In reality, travel photography is not really a single genre of photography but rather an amalgamation of several genres. It is people photography, documentary, landscape, reportage, wildlife, architectural, still-life, abstract and more. But none of this really matters, the labels aren't important. What is evident is that travel photography can take credit for many of the finest and most engaging contemporary images.

That time has arrived again, the time to start turning the pages and discovering new worlds and new visions of familiar ones. It's a journey like no other...

TRAVEL PHOTOGRAPHER OF THE YEAR 2013

The Cutty Sark Award

The power of story telling combined with the magical qualities of black and white photography won Timothy Allen the Cutty Sark Award and the title of Travel Photographer of the Year. With four of his portfolios shortlisted in different categories, the judges were impressed by the consistently outstanding standard of Timothy's entry, finding his imagery noteworthy, engaging and well paced, but it was the two black and white portfolios which really caught the eye. Both shot in Mali, one tells the story of a communal festival to re-plaster the Great Mosque of Djenné - La Fete de Crépissage. The other gives a glimpse into a Dogon community.

Sponsors of this award:
Cutty Sark Blended Scotch Whisky

Djenné, Mali. **Timothy Allen, UK.** *Canon 5D II with 16-35mm lens; f5.6; 1/500s; ISO 640*

Djenné, Mali. **Timothy Allen, UK.** *Canon 5D II with 16–35mm lens; f2.8; 1/16s; ISO 1600*

Djenné, Mali. **Timothy Allen, UK.** *Canon 5D II with 16–35mm lens; f5; 1/500s; ISO 640*

TRAVEL PHOTOGRAPHER OF THE YEAR 2013

Timothy Allen UK
Winner
The Cutty Sark Award

Every year, Djenné celebrates La Fete de Crépissage – the plastering of the city's central mosque. It is the largest mud building in the world and, for one day, men and boys collect mud (adobe) in small baskets from locations just outside the city and apply it to the walls of the Great Mosque amid a vibrant festival atmosphere.

Djenné, Mali. **Timothy Allen, UK.** *Canon 5D II with 85mm lens; f1.4; 1/3200s; ISO 200*

Dogon Country, Mali. **Timothy Allen, UK.** *Canon 5D MkII with 200mm lens; f9; 1/1000s; ISO 640*

Dogon Country, Mali. **Timothy Allen, UK.**
Canon 5D II with 16–35mm lens; f2.8; 1/16s; ISO 1600

TRAVEL PHOTOGRAPHER
OF THE YEAR 2013

Timothy Allen UK
Winner
The Cutty Sark Award

Above. Dogon women walk across the sand to their village. Dogon country has been classified as a UNESCO World Heritage Site because of its rich culture.

Left. Men sharing the meat from a sacrificial ceremony. Over the years, I've been present at quite a few blood offerings and the one thing I continue to find interesting is how this initially unsavoury experience quickly turns into something highly sociable and welcoming. It also makes me question my reasons for being a vegetarian – it seems to be in direct conflict with my animal nature.

Dogon Country, Mali. **Timothy Allen, UK.** *Canon 5D MkII with 200mm lens; f2.8; 1/250s; ISO 640*

Above. A Dogon woman shelters from the rain beneath the pointed, thatched roof of a traditional mud-wall granary in a Dogon village near the Bandiagara Escarpment.

Right. Dogon Country is steeped in supernatural rules and age-old do's and don'ts thanks to the culture's tumultuous history and their attempts to master their unforgiving environment. As a result, our protective neighbours closely scrutinized our every step to ensure we didn't make a faux pas.

Dogon Country, Mali. **Timothy Allen, UK.**
Canon 5D II with 85mm lens; f2; 1/1328s; ISO 640

YOUNG TRAVEL PHOTOGRAPHER OF THE YEAR 2013

Crowded Planet

The young photographers continue to make images which show a different perspective on the world and it is both inspiring and encouraging that so many young people engage with photography in such a creative way. In his winning portfolio, Jonathan Rystrøm's experiments with movement give a refreshingly different insight into a crowded place, very much from a young person's perspective.

Sponsors of this award:

Fujifilm, Plastic Sandwich, TPOTY

Dubrovnik, Croatia. **Jonathan Rystrøm, Denmark (age 14).** *Canon EOS 60D with 18–135mm lens; f16; 1/10s; ISO 100*

Dubrovnik, Croatia. **Jonathan Rystrøm, Denmark (age 14).** *Canon EOS 60D with 18–135mm lens; f10; 8s; ISO 100*

YOUNG TRAVEL PHOTOGRAPHER OF THE YEAR 2013

Jonathan Rystrøm Denmark
Winner

Previous page. I was sitting at a café resting in between shots when I got the idea for this picture. It was very interesting just watching all the busy tourists walking by. I wanted to also get another perspective on the tourists of Dubrovnik to create diversity in the series.

Right. In this picture I wanted to convey the fact that it isn't only on the main street that it is busy. There are lots of tourists everywhere in Dubrovnik. The picture was taken in the afternoon when the light still was harsh. Therefore I had to use a neutral density filter so I could get the long exposure.

Dubrovnik, Croatia. **Jonathan Rystrøm, Denmark (age 14).**
Canon EOS 60D with 18–135mm lens; f13; 8s; ISO 100

Dubrovnik, Croatia. **Jonathan Rystrøm, Denmark (age 14).** *Canon EOS 60D with 18–135mm lens; f22; 2.5s; ISO 100*

This picture is taken right in the start of The Strada. It is the place where thousands of tourists arrive and try to get the first impressions of the amazing medieval city. It amazed me how busy everyone was – maybe because the majority of the tourists have to see Dubrovnik in only five hours before cruising on to Venice or Split. The sun was shining so I used a neutral density filter to allow for long exposure.

Opposite page, top. Dubrovnik is an old medieval city, which is very busy in the summer, with thousands of cruise tourists every day. I used a long exposure, so the moving tourists appear blurry, while the man, who is sitting still, remains sharp. The picture focuses on the contrast between movement and relaxation. It is important to remember that, even in the busiest places, there is always room for a moment of calmness. This was the photo that gave me the idea for the rest of the series.

New York City, USA. **Chase Guttman, USA (age 17).** *Nikon D50 with 12–24mm lens; f4; 1/125s; ISO 400*

YOUNG TRAVEL PHOTOGRAPHER OF THE YEAR 2013

Chase Guttman USA
Winner - 15-18 age group

Left. An ebullient crowd of bubble gun-toting combatants compete in front of excited spectators in Times Square – one of the busiest pedestrian intersections in the world.

Right. Hordes of mischievous Santas assemble at Bethseda Terrace in Central Park for the annual Santacon bar crawl.

Below. A snowstorm of feathers fills the air during a pillow fight held in New York's Union Square.

Below right. Camouflaged training battalions spiral into tight formation at the historic Virginia Military Institute. Founded in 1839, this military school played an integral role in the Civil War, with many of its graduates rising to the rank of General. One of its alumni, Benjamin Franklin Ficklin, went on to found the Pony Express.

New York City, USA. **Chase Guttman, USA (age 17).**
Nikon D50 with 12–24mm lens; f6.3; 1/160s; ISO 200

New York City, USA. **Chase Guttman, USA (age 17).**
Nikon D50 with 28–80mm lens; f3.3; 1/2500s; ISO 200

Lexington, Virginia, USA. **Chase Guttman, USA (age 17).**
Nikon D50 with 28–80mm lens; f3.3; 1/40s; ISO 200

Surabaya, Indonesia. **Patria Prasasya, Indonesia (age 10).**
Canon 1100D with 18–55mm lens; f16; 1/125s; ISO 1600

Surabaya, Indonesia. **Patria Prasasya, Indonesia (age 10).**
Canon 1100D with 18–55mm lens; f16; 1/125s; ISO 1600

Above left. To photograph ants outside my house, I threw pieces of bread onto the ground and waited for them to arrive.

Above right. Near the bread, I saw a red ant fighting with a smaller black one. I thought the black ant would easily lose, but other black ants came to help it.

Right. Other black ants continued to arrive and encircle the larger red ant.

Surabaya, Indonesia. **Patria Prasasya, Indonesia (age 10).** *Canon 1100D with 18–55mm lens; f16; 1/125s; ISO 1600*

YOUNG TRAVEL PHOTOGRAPHER OF THE YEAR 2013

Patria Prasasya Indonesia
Winner - under 14 age group

Below. The original black ant became exhausted, but the remaining black ants continued to fight with the outnumbered red ant.

Surabaya, Indonesia. **Patria Prasasya, Indonesia (age 10).** *Canon 1100D with 18–55mm lens; f16; 1/125s; ISO 1600*

Bhaktapur, Nepal. **Jovian Salak, UK (age 18).** *Nikon D800 with 21mm lens; f2.8; 1/400s; ISO 320*

YOUNG TRAVEL PHOTOGRAPHER OF THE YEAR 2013

Jovian Salak UK
Runner Up - 15-18 age group

Above. A young boy monitors a crowded chariot wheel during Bisket Jatra – the Nepali New Year festival. The chariot takes on the role of a portable shrine, with eggs being broken and a chicken sacrificed upon it. It is then dragged through the streets amid huge, excited crowds.

Right. A very tall ceremonial pole is raised and competitors race to climb the ropes and put some money at the top before the police arrive. It is said the lucky few that manage to do so will be granted a son and lots of money.

Bhaktapur, Nepal. **Jovian Salak, UK (age 18).**
Nikon D300 with 70mm lens; f2.8; 1/800s; ISO 400

Mara River, North Serengeti, Tanzania. **Myriam Deckmyn, Belgium (age 12).**
Sony HX 50V compact; f6.3; 1/250s; ISO 100

YOUNG TRAVEL PHOTOGRAPHER OF THE YEAR 2013

Myriam Deckmyn Belgium
Runner Up - under 14 age group

Every August, millions of wildebeest cross the Mara River in Tanzania to reach Kenya's lush grazing grounds, which crop up after the rains. Vultures fill the air and crocodiles patrol the waters, waiting to pounce on the struggling wildebeest.

Mara River, North Serengeti, Tanzania. **Myriam Deckmyn, Belgium (age 12).** *Sony HX 50V compact; f6.3; 1/250s; ISO 100*

VANISHING AND EMERGING CULTURES PORTFOLIO 2013

Travel photography reflects both the traditional cultures, which are increasingly under threat, and those which are emerging alongside them. In Gavin Gough's winning portfolio of skateboarders in Kolkata, India, an old and decaying building presents the backdrop for a vibrant and energetic youth culture, capturing the vitality, pride and reflectiveness of the young in an engaging and colourful set of images.

Sponsors of this award:

Fujifilm, Genesis Imaging, Plastic Sandwich, Royal Geographical Society (with IBG)

Kolkata Skateboarding Club, Kolkata, West Bengal, India. **Gavin Gough, UK.** *Canon EOS 5D MkIII with 16–35mm lens; f2.8; 1/60s; ISO 100*

Kolkata Skateboarding Club, Kolkata, West Bengal, India. **Gavin Gough, UK.** *Canon EOS 5D MkIII with 16–35mm lens; f2.8; 1/60s; ISO 1600*

VANISHING AND EMERGING CULTURES PORTFOLIO 2013

Gavin Gough UK
Winner

Previous page. One of the children participating in the Kolkata Skateboarding project leaps excitedly through a window in the abandoned warehouse where weekly classes take place.

Above. As well as learning to skateboard, children at the Kolkata Skateboarding project enjoy the opportunity to learn hip-hop dance moves from a visiting volunteer.

Kolkata Skateboarding Club, Kolkata, West Bengal, India. **Gavin Gough, UK.**
Canon EOS 5D MkIII with 16–35mm lens; f2.8; 1/60s; ISO 200

Above right. One of the children participating in the Kolkata Skateboarding project waits for the weekly session to begin at an abandoned warehouse. The Kolkata Skateboarding project was created by Aaron and Debora Walling and provides children from disadvantaged communities in Kolkata with an opportunity to learn new skills, building upon teamwork and self-discipline. The initiative is proving to be both greatly entertaining and rewarding for students and teachers alike.

Right. One of the participants at the Kolkata Skateboarding project stands proudly with the skateboard, helmet, gloves and pads provided by the initiative.

Kolkata Skateboarding Club, Kolkata, West Bengal, India. **Gavin Gough, UK.**
Canon EOS 5D MkIII with 16–35mm lens; f2.8; 1/60s; ISO 100

Alti region, Western Mongolia. **Simon Morris, UK.** *Nikon D700 with 28–70mm lens; f11; 1/60s; ISO 200*

Alti region, Western Mongolia. **Simon Morris, UK.** *Nikon D700 with 28–70mm lens; f11; 1/125s; ISO 200*

Alti region, Western Mongolia. **Simon Morris, UK.**
Nikon D700 with 28–70mm lens; f5.6; 1/60s; ISO 200

Alti region, Western Mongolia. **Simon Morris, UK.**
Nikon D700 with 50mm lens; f4.2; 1/125s; ISO 200

VANISHING AND EMERGING CULTURES PORTFOLIO 2013

Simon Morris UK
Runner Up

Opposite page. Mr Ardak resting next to his Golden Eagle. The hunters raise their birds from young and when they are too old to hunt, the birds are set free and another eagle obtained. Only female eagles are chosen because they are bigger and more aggressive.

Above left. Mongolian eagle hunters treat their eagles as part of the family; loving and caring for them tenderly. I stayed with the hunters and their families for three weeks and shot this image of Mr Ardak, resting on the ice with his Golden Eagle, in the late afternoon after a morning hunting furs.

Above. The picture demonstrates how close the Mongolians are to their birds – the young lad had no fear at all of approaching the eagle and used to feed it with his grandfather present.

Left. Eagle hunters hunt mainly for furs. It is an ancient art that has been passed down from the great khans of old.

VANISHING AND EMERGING CULTURES PORTFOLIO 2013

Jason Edwards Australia
Highly Commended

Camels launch from the start gate, whipped to speed by
their 'jockeys'.

North of Wahiba Sands, Oman. **Jason Edwards, Australia.** *Nikon D700 with 14–24mm lens; f2.8; 1/2000s; ISO 200*

Far right. Trainers and owners prepare their robotic jockeys ahead of the race.

Right. Innovations in technology now allow camels to be ridden by robotic jockeys instead of child jockeys. Here, a camel handler struggles to control his charge as they proceed to the starting gate.

Below. Camels race to the finish line, while large crowds cheer from the sidelines.

North of Wahiba Sands, Oman. **Jason Edwards, Australia.**
Nikon D700 with 14–24mm lens; f2.8; 1/2000s; ISO 200

North of Wahiba Sands, Oman. **Jason Edwards, Australia.**
Nikon D700 with 14–24mm lens; f2.8; 1/1000s; ISO 200

North of Wahiba Sands, Oman. **Jason Edwards, Australia.** *Nikon D700 with 200–400mm lens; f4; 1/2500s; ISO 200*

Andaman Sea. **Cat Vinton, UK.** *Canon EOS 1DS MkIII with 24–105mm lens; f10; 1/200s; ISO 160*

Andaman Sea. **Cat Vinton, UK.** *Canon EOS 1DS MkIII with 24–105mm lens; f4.5; 3.2s; ISO 400*

VANISHING AND EMERGING CULTURES PORTFOLIO 2013

Cat Vinton UK
Commended

Above. The Moken harvest the sea's bounty with harpoons, hands and nets. They have incredible underwater vision – it's believed to be twice as sharp as 'ours' – and Moken children can swim before they can walk.

Left. The Moken have no word for 'want'. Their kabang boats are decorated with identical scroll designs on the bow and stern to symbolise the mouth-to-exit digestion process that holds onto nothing permanently.

Amazon rainforest, Amazonas, Brazil. **David Lazar, Australia.** *Nikon D700 with 24–85mm lens; f5.6; 1/125s; ISO 320*

Amazon rainforest, Amazonas, Brazil. **David Lazar, Australia.**
Nikon D700 with 24–85mm lens; f5.6; 1/125s; ISO 640

VANISHING AND EMERGING CULTURES PORTFOLIO 2013

David Lazar Australia
Commended

Above. Portrait of a Dessana chief in a village on the Amazon River. He wears traditional face paint and a full Macaw feather headdress.

Left. A baby born in the rainforest is cared for by his mother and grandmother. Family and community play an important role in the raising of an Amazonian child.

MONOCHROMAL PORTFOLIO 2013

 There is a magic about monochrome that defies time and selecting the winner of this category was no easy task. The sheer variety of entries is evident in the diversity of imagery on the following pages. Jino Lee's images of a Chinese boat fisherman are elegant in their simplicity, subtle tonality and exquisite mood. The reflections and swirling mist add to the atmosphere of these beautiful images.

Sponsors of this award:

Yosemite/Mariposa County Tourism Bureau, San Francisco Travel, Sonoma County Tourism Bureau, Genesis Imaging, Plastic Sandwich, Royal Geographical Society (with IBG)

Dongjiang Lake, Hunan, China. **Jino Lee, Malaysia.** *Canon EOS 1DX with 24–105mm lens; f8; 1/500s; ISO 400*

Dongjiang Lake, Hunan, China. **Jino Lee, Malaysia.** *Canon EOS 1DX with 24–105mm lens; f10; 1/500s; ISO 400*

MONOCHROMAL
PORTFOLIO 2013

Jino Lee Malaysia
Winner

The fishermen on the Dongjiang Lake work only a few hours a day, usually very early in the morning and late in the afternoon. The challenge of photographing them well is capturing them in the right conditions, but all too frequently it was too misty, too cloudy, or too bright. And even when the light and mist were ideal, the fishermen needed to be in the right spot in order to complete the picture.

During those four days – and many hours of trying – all three elements fell into place on only two occasions, but it was worth the wait! I'm really pleased with the results.

Dongjiang Lake, Hunan, China. **Jino Lee, Malaysia.** *Canon EOS 1DX with Canon 24–105mm lens; f8; 1/640s; ISO 400*

Dongjiang Lake, Hunan, China. **Jino Lee, Malaysia.** *Canon EOS 1DX with 24–105mm lens; f8; 1/500s; ISO 400*

Gullfoss waterfall, Iceland. **Emmanuel Coupe, France.**
Canon D800E with 21mm lens; f8; 30s; ISO 200

Vík coast, Iceland. **Emmanuel Coupe, France.**
Canon D800E with 100mm lens; f8; 60s; ISO 100

Opposite page. Skógafoss waterfall, South Iceland. **Emmanuel Coupe, France.**
Canon D800E with 70–200mm lens; f9; 30s; ISO 200

Hvítserkur, Iceland. **Emmanuel Coupe, France.**
Canon D800E with 21mm lens; f8; 30s; ISO 100

MONOCHROMAL PORTFOLIO 2013

Emmanuel Coupe France
Runner Up

Top left. There was not a soul to be seen when I visited Gullfoss waterfall one October day. The spray coming from the fall made it seem as if a rainstorm was present.

Above. I was drawn to the unique shape and texture of this rock. I made several return visits to the location; observing the tides and light and considering which conditions would best suit my photographic vision of this place. In the end, the reflective water of a mid-tide gave the rock the presence I was after.

Left. I spent several days around the shores of southern Iceland and was faced with strong winds that at times made it impossible to stand up, let alone set up a tripod. Although seemingly rather peaceful, this photo was taken under such extreme conditions.

Opposite page. Iceland's Skógafoss waterfall is a commanding presence, with the roaring water dropping a furious 60 metres. My approach to this scenery was to bring forth the stark contrasts and simple elegance of the landscape.

MONOCHROMAL PORTFOLIO 2013

Beniamino Pisati Italy
Highly Commended

Right. The milking of cows is still carried out manually and the valleys echo with the signs and symbols of a traditional pastoral world.

Below. Bitto cheese has ancient origins that are rooted in the Alpine area of Valle del Bitto di Albaredo and Gerola, right in the heart of Italy's Parco delle Orobie Valtellinesi. The production process lasts four months and is conducted at over 1500m.

Valtellina, Lombardy, Italy. **Beniamino Pisati, Italy.** *Canon 5D MkII with 16–35mm lens; f2.8; 1/1250s; ISO 200*

Valtellina, Lombardy, Italy. **Beniamino Pisati, Italy.** *Canon 5D MkII with 70–200mm lens; f5.6; 1/250s; ISO 400*

Valtellina, Lombardy, Italy. **Beniamino Pisati, Italy.**
Canon 5D MkII with 24–105mm lens; f4; 1/30s; ISO 2500

Valtellina, Lombardy, Italy. **Beniamino Pisati, Italy.**
Canon 5D MkII with 16–35mm lens; f5; 1/80s; ISO 1000

Left. The cheese starts to ripen in the Alpine 'casera' – a small rural hut not far from the pastures – and finishes in the factories down the valley. Bitto is the only cheese in the world which can be left to ripen for more than ten years.

Above. To make Bitto cheese, cows' milk is mixed with goats' milk and poured into traditional copper vats, shaped like upturned bells. Within two hours, it is warmed to its final temperature, removed from the copper and placed into wooden containers.

Amaya village, East Pokot, Kenya. **Roberto Nistri, Italy.** *Nikon D300S with 70–200mm lens; f22; 1/180s; ISO 200*

MONOCHROMAL PORTFOLIO 2013

Roberto Nistri Italy
Commended

The Pokot tribe inhabits the arid, inhospitable wilds of northern Kenya. When women and men performed a spectacular 'war dance' – moving between bonfires and thick clouds of smoke lit by a relentless sun – it was clear to me that they were intimately connected to their land.

Amaya village, East Pokot, Kenya. **Roberto Nistri, Italy.** *Nikon D300S with 12–24mm lens; f4; 1/3000s; ISO 200*

WILD STORIES
PORTFOLIO 2013

For the first time ever, TPOTY had joint winners in a portfolio category – and they could not be more different. Jasper Doest's stunning portraits of Japanese macaques are both elegant and intimate, all boldly and unusually portrayed with their eyes closed. In stark contrast, Johnny Haglund's portfolio is both gritty and disturbing, telling a poignant story of a brutal family business with intense insight and from close proximity.

Sponsors of this award:

TPOTY, Genesis Imaging, Plastic Sandwich, Royal Geographical Society (with IBG)

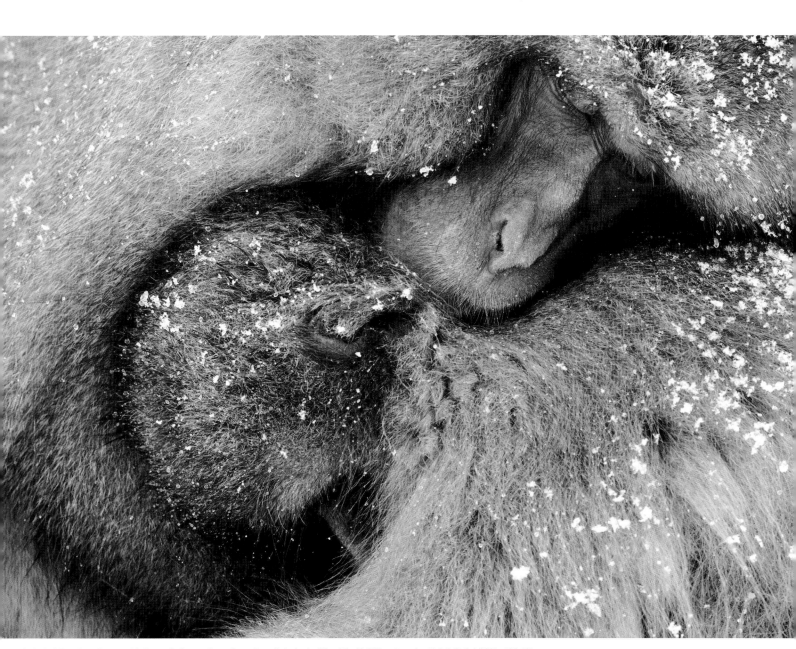

Jigokudani Yaen Koen, Yamanouchi, Nagano Prefecture, Japan. **Jasper Doest, Netherlands.** *Nikon D3 with 300mm lens plus TC 1.4; f5.6; 1/1000s; ISO 400*

WILD STORIES
PORTFOLIO 2013

Jasper Doest Netherlands
Joint Winner

Previous page. Bathing in the hotsprings has become a social bonding activity for the whole troop.

Right. The Japanese macaques discovered they could stay warm by bathing in the natural hotsprings that occur in the snowy Jigokudani mountains. Now, some decades later, they not only bathe on a daily basis, but there are signs the intelligent monkeys have adapted to this aquatic environment.

Below. Japanese macaque huddling with her baby to stay warm during a blizzard.

Opposite page. Jigokudani Yean-Koen literally means 'Hell's Valley', but for the macaques that live there, it's heaven on earth. It is the only place in the world where you can observe and photograph Japanese macaques up close in their natural habitat, like this snow-covered sleeping juvenile.

Jigokudani Yaen Koen, Yamanouchi, Nagano Prefecture, Japan. **Jasper Doest, Netherlands.**
Nikon D3 with 70–200mm lens; f16; 1/13s; ISO 640

Jigokudani Yaen Kōen, Yamanouchi, Nagano Prefecture, Japan. **Jasper Doest, Netherlands.**
Nikon D3 with 70–200mm lens; f11; 1/100s; ISO 1000

Jigokudani Yaen Kōen, Yamanouchi, Nagano Prefecture, Japan. **Jasper Doest, Netherlands.**
Nikon D3 with 105mm lens; f16; 1/200s; ISO 2000

Lac des Allemands, Louisiana, USA. **Johnny Haglund, Norway.** *Canon EOS 1Dx with 16-35mm lens; f20; 1/160s; ISO 1600*

WILD STORIES
PORTFOLIO 2013

Johnny Haglund Norway
Joint Winner

Above. Ed and his friend, Eugene, have hunted alligators since the ban was abolished in 1981. In this photograph, Ed stands ready to kill the next catch while his five year-old grandson watches with curiosity. He told me he wants to be an alligator hunter when he grows up.

Right. After a long day in the swamps, Ed and Eugene offload the day's catch: eight alligators. Ed's 11 year-old grandaugher looks on. She too wants to be an alligator hunter when she grows up.

Louisiana, USA. **Johnny Haglund, Norway.**
Canon EOS 1Dx with 24–70mm lens; f18; 1/160s; ISO 400

Lac des Allemands, Louisiana, USA. **Johnny Haglund, Norway.** *Canon EOS 1Dx with 16–35mm lens; f22; 1/160s; ISO 400*

Lac des Allemands, Louisiana, USA. **Johnny Haglund, Norway.**
Canon EOS 1Dx with 16–35mm lens; f22; 1/20s; ISO 200

Above. Ed's grandson has already shot several alligators. It was strange for me to see such a young child with a gun, but his grandfather was very careful about teaching him how to use and handle it correctly.

Left. Ed and two of his grandchildren cruising through the swamps looking for alligators. A previous kill lies in the bottom of the boat. To catch one, Ed puts bait on a solid hook and attaches it to a nearby tree. When the hook gets stuck inside the alligator's belly, the hunters pull the string and the angry beast surfaces. They then pull it towards the boat and quickly put a bullet in its head.

Chief's Island, Okavango Delta, Botswana. **Ed Hetherington, USA.**
Canon 5D MkIII with 100–400mm lens; f5.6; 1/1000s; ISO 640

Chief's Island, Okavango Delta, Botswana. **Ed Hetherington, USA.**
Canon 5D MkIII with 300mm lens; f5; 1/640s; ISO 250

Chief's Island, Okavango Delta, Botswana. **Ed Hetherington, USA.**
Canon 5D MkIII with 100–400mm lens; f6.3; 1/3200s; ISO 800

WILD STORIES PORTFOLIO 2013

Ed Hetherington USA
Runner Up

Top left. When watching the lionesses sleep earlier in the morning, their paws looked almost soft and cuddly, but this image shows just how lethal their retractable claws are.

Top right. During the hunt, the pride worked as a cohesive team with perfect cooperation, but when the time came to eat there were plenty of disagreements as the most dominant members of the pride staked their claims to the best pieces of the carcass.

Left. Members of the Mathatha pride line up to begin a hunt. We followed them during the morning as they marched single file across their territory. When they sensed a herd of buffalo nearby, they would stop briefly, with each lioness scanning in a slightly different direction.

Below. The lionesses discovered a lone buffalo that had wandered too far from the safety of his herd. It took teamwork to bring down the large animal. The struggle was violent and the seemingly calm scene in this image happened for only a split second.

Chief's Island, Okavango Delta, Botswana. **Ed Hetherington, USA.** *Canon 5D MkIII with 100–400mm lens; f5; 1/2000s; ISO 640*

Castelluccio di Norcia, Italy. **Barbara Dall'Angelo, Italy.** *Nikon D300S with 70–200mm lens; f16; 1/25s; ISO 250*

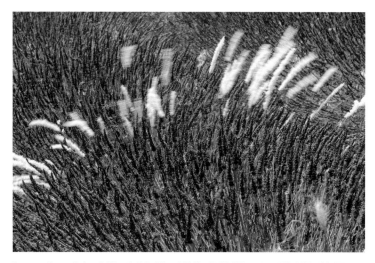

Provence, France. **Barbara Dall'Angelo, Italy.** *Nikon D300S with 70–200mm lens; f20; 1/15s; ISO 200*

WILD STORIES
PORTFOLIO 2013

Barbara Dall'Angelo Italy
Highly Commended

Top. Seen from a distance, this field of red poppies, yellow cornflowers and rapeseed flowers reminded me of a Pointillist painting and I wanted to convey the same abstract feeling in my photograph.

Left. Lavender fields in Provence perfectly capture the mood of summer.

Abruzzo, Italy. **Barbara Dall'Angelo, Italy.** *Nikon D800 with 70–200mm lens; f2.8; 1/80s; ISO 200*

Above. A touch of autumn taken in Abruzzo National Park. I chose a wide aperture to give the image a softer look.

Right. I wanted to capture the essence of each season through its characteristic colours. Snow falls rarely in Rome, so when I woke up one morning to see everything covered in white, I immediately grabbed my camera and took this shot from my window.

Rome, Italy. **Barbara Dall'Angelo, Italy.** *Canon EOS 5D MkII with 70–200mm lens; f4.4; 1/80s; ISO 200*

Mount Kent, Falkland Islands. **Tim Taylor, UK.**
Canon EOS 5D MkII with 16–35mm lens; f22; 1s; ISO 50

WILD STORIES
PORTFOLIO 2013

Tim Taylor UK
Commended

Left. The remote location of the Falkland Islands means that many remnants of war remain frozen in time, like this Argentine Chinook helicopter, at rest in a peat bog.

Below. A lenticular cloud sits above the mountains surrounding the remote settlement of Goose Green. On 4th May 1982, my uncle was shot down and killed while flying his Sea Harrier over this sound during the Falklands War.

Goose Green, Falkland Islands. **Tim Taylor, UK.** *Canon EOS 5D MkII with 24–105mm lens; f22; 0.3s; ISO 50*

Mohammadi, Lakhimpur Kheri, Uttar Pradesh, India. **Satpal Singh, India.** *Nikon D90 with 105mm VR Micro lens; f13; 1/100s; ISO 200*

Mohammadi, Lakhimpur Kheri, Uttar Pradesh, India. **Satpal Singh, India.** *Nikon D90 with 105mm VR Micro lens; f13; 1/200s; ISO 200*

WILD STORIES
PORTFOLIO 2013

Satpal Singh India
Commended

Above. Weaver ants get their name from their amazing stitching skills: a number of leaves are stretched into position, held in placc by row upon row of workers and then stitched together to create a nest.

Left. Whenever an ant gets injured, healthy ones assist it back to the nest, holding it delicately by its petiole or neck during the transfer process.

ONE SHOT 2013
EXTRAORDINARY

If ever there was a need to affirm what an extraordinary world we live in, then you can find it here. With such a conceptual theme it was inevitable that the subject matter would be diverse and this is evident in the winning images, which ranged from the mesmerisingly beautiful to the unbelievably tragic. Justin Mott's winning image plays tricks on the mind and captures two worlds with serene beauty and elegance, whilst leaving the viewer wondering 'how did he do that?'

Sponsors of this award:

cazenove+loyd

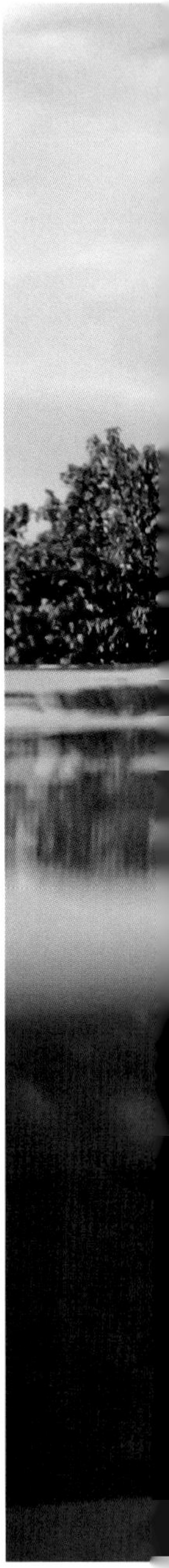

Phuket, Thailand. **Justin Mott, USA.** *Canon EOS 5D Mk I; f22; 1/200s; ISO 500*

ONE SHOT 2013
EXTRAORDINARY

Justin Mott USA
Winner

Previous page. This image puzzles people. 'Why aren't the elephant's legs visible if it's swimming in the same pool as the girl?' they ask. The answer is very simple: the elephant isn't in the water at all! The girl is swimming in a very large above-ground pool, while the elephant is standing on solid ground behind it. To take the shot, I had to get into the pool and dip my camera – covered in a waterproof bag – half in and half out of the water. The reflection of the animal's trunk and body in the water makes it look like a cohesive image.

French Alps. **Tim Taylor, UK.** *Canon EOS 5D MkII with 100–400mm lens; f22; 1/13s; ISO 50*

ONE SHOT 2013
EXTRAORDINARY

Tim Taylor UK
Runner Up

The image was taken in the early morning, just as the moon was setting. This meant that the exposure could be reduced enough to pull detail out of the landscape without blowing out the highlights of the moon and losing the detail of its pockmarked surface.

Chobe National Park, Botswana. **Jason Edwards, Australia.** *Nikon D3S with 14-24mm lens; f2.8; 1/500s; ISO 400*

ONE SHOT 2013
EXTRAORDINARY

Jason Edwards Australia
Runner Up

The tortured and charred remains of an African elephant rest beside
a road in northern Botswana. The animal was originally slaughtered
for bushmeat, but the poachers were disturbed before they could
dismember the carcass. National Park rangers torched the remains
after discerning the elephant was contaminated with anthrax.

Tarragona, Catalonia, Spain. **David Oliete, Spain.** *Canon 7D with 24–105mm lens; f4; 1/160s; ISO 160*

ONE SHOT 2013
EXTRAORDINARY

David Oliete Spain
Highly Commended

The UNESCO-listed Human Towers competition takes place every two years in Tarragona. Part of Catalan cultural tradition for more than 200 years, teams of between 100 and 500 men and women race to build the highest human tower possible.

ONE SHOT 2013 EXTRAORDINARY

Nicolas Lotsos Greece
Commended

Light was fading on the Kenyan savanna and we were ready to return to camp when, suddenly, we spotted this beautiful leopard that had just climbed up the tree to settle for his night vigil.

Masai Mara, Kenya. **Nicolas Lotsos, Greece.** *Nikon D800E with 70–200mm lens; f2.8; 1/500s; ISO 1600*

ONE SHOT 2013
EXTRAORDINARY

Gerald Baeck Austria
Commended

The ongoing monsoon season demonstrates its explosive power over the north rim of the Grand Canyon on a late August afternoon. Minutes later the thunderstorm changed direction and we had to evacuate the platform.

Grand Canyon, USA. **Gerald Baeck, Austria.** *Pentax K7 with 50mm lens; f22; 2s; ISO 100*

Masai Mara, Kenya. **David Lazar, Australia.** *Nikon D700 with 24–85mm lens; f7.1; 1/200s; ISO 400*

ONE SHOT 2013
EXTRAORDINARY

David Lazar Australia
Commended

Early one morning, we came across these two lionesses out walking with a tiny lion cub. The cub was much smaller and less adventurous than its siblings, preferring to stay close to the lionesses.

ONE SHOT 2013
EXTRAORDINARY

Marco Urso Italy
Special Mention

I followed this cheetah and her cub for two days to achieve this shot. Late on the second day, the cub climbed this termite nest and started licking its mother. We're used to seeing a mother's love for its child, but here we see the opposite as well.

Masai Mara, Kenya. **Marco Urso, Italy.** *Canon EOS DX1 with 44mm lens; f4.5; 1/320s; ISO 160*

ONE SHOT 2013
EXTRAORDINARY

Judith Conning Australia
Special Mention

The Milky Way mingles with the lights of Mercedes Cove Coastal Retreat, in Western Australia. Whales pass through the azure seas during migration season and I could hear them splashing their huge flippers as I took this photo.

Mercedes Cove, Western Australia. **Judith Conning, Australia.** *Canon 5D MkII with 14mm lens; f2; 15s; ISO 6400*

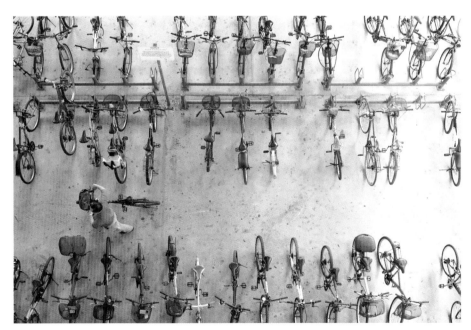

ONE SHOT 2013
EXTRAORDINARY

Kokkai Ng Singapore
Special Mention

Bird's eye view of a man pushing his bicycle out of Boon Lay MRT Station.

Jurong West, Singapore. **Kokkai Ng, Singapore.** *Sony A330 with 18–55mm lens; f4.5; 1/100s; ISO 400*

NEW TALENT 2013
METROPOLIS

Over the years the New Talent category has uncovered some wonderful raw talent amongst aspiring photographers, many of whom are now going on to realise their dream career in photography. The skill of storytelling through pictures is a key tool for any professional photographer and the judges look for this quality within the portfolios. Winner, Tom Pepper, tackles a well-known and much photographed city with a portfolio of both vibrant and subtle images, capturing the essence of Metropolis - no easy task in a city where we feel we've seen it all before.

Sponsors of this award:

Fujifilm, Photo Iconic, Plastic Sandwich

New York City, USA. **Tom Pepper, UK**. *Nikon D800 with 16–35mm lens; f11; 30s; ISO 100*

New York City, USA. **Tom Pepper, UK.** *Nikon D800 with 16–35mm lens; f20; 30s; ISO 50*

NEW TALENT 2013
METROPOLIS

Tom Pepper UK
Winner

Previous page. This image shows the Manhattan skyline at sunset, with the Brooklyn Bridge stretching across the water connecting the two boroughs. I crouched at the tideline and set the camera upon my tripod at a deliberately low angle so as to include the rocks in the foreground, which nicely balance the fragmented clouds passing above New York.

Above. This stark image is intended to represent the quintessential metropolis: highly developed, brimming with imposing architecture, futuristic, and active whatever the time of day. I initially got the settings slightly wrong and overexposed the sky, but I liked the effect and pushed the exposure further until the sky was completely white and additional detail was visible in the buildings of the skyline.

New York City, USA. **Tom Pepper, UK.**
Nikon D800 with 16–35mm lens; f4; 1/20s; ISO 125

New York City, USA. **Tom Pepper, UK.**
Nikon D800 with 16–35mm lens; f11; 1/15s; ISO 100

New York City, USA. **Tom Pepper, UK.**
Nikon D800 with 16–35mm lens; f16; 30s; ISO 50

Top left. Originally the location of the New York Times headquarters, Times Square is said to be the most-visited tourist attraction in the world. No trip to New York is complete without experiencing it. The iconic illuminated signs emit enough light to allow night photography at daytime settings!

Centre left. The main subject of this image – The Flatiron Building – is considered to be one of the first skyscrapers in New York City. I used a slow shutter speed to convey the bustle of the area and continuous flow of canary-yellow taxis and, to get above the crowds, I stood on a conveniently placed rock!

Bottom left. This distinctive Art Deco terminal was refurbished in 2005. Each day, the ferries transport approximately 75,000 passengers to and from Staten Island. It's popular with tourists because it passes close to the Statue of Liberty and is free! In order to capture the movement of the people and clouds, I used a dark filter on the lens and a correspondingly long shutter speed.

Below. The medallion required to operate an official New York taxicab – they currently sell for more than US$1 million apiece! The taxi was passing the US Armed Forces Recruiting Station in Times Square, the illuminated American flag of which is reflected in its steel bonnet.

New York City, USA. **Tom Pepper, UK.**
Nikon D800 with 28-300mm lens; f5.6; 1/125s; ISO 320

Grand Central Station, New York City, USA. **Sheng Hong Tan, Malaysia.**
Canon EOS 5D with 40mm lens; f3.5; 1/200s; ISO 1250

Grand Central Station, New York City, USA. **Sheng Hong Tan, Malaysia.**
Canon EOS 5D with 40mm lens; f3.5; 1/200s; ISO 1250

Grand Central Station, New York City, USA. **Sheng Hong Tan, Malaysia.**
Canon EOS 5D with 40mm lens; f3.2; 1/200s; ISO 1250

Grand Central Station, New York City, USA. **Sheng Hong Tan, Malaysia.**
Canon EOS 5D with 40mm lens; f3.5; 1/160s; ISO 640

Grand Central Station, New York City, USA. **Sheng Hong Tan, Malaysia.**
Canon EOS 5D with 40mm lens; f3.2; 1/160s; ISO 800

Grand Central Station, New York City, USA. **Sheng Hong Tan, Malaysia.** *Canon EOS 5D with 40mm lens; f3.5; 1/125s; ISO 1000*

NEW TALENT 2013
METROPOLIS

Sheng Hong Tan Malaysia
Runner Up

New York City is known the world over for its brutal honesty and eclectic diversity. But sometimes these distinctions and differences collapse. Exits and entrances become one. Mothers, lovers, and labourers become one. Friend and foe become one. There is nothing but the singular devotion towards making it through yet another obstacle.

These images aim to capture New Yorkers at such a moment, as they attempt to push through turnstiles at a New York institution – the Grand Central Terminal. Amid the hustle and bustle, they contemplate, for an instant, the photographer's gaze, before stepping back into the hurricane of their lives.

Brick Lane, London, UK. **Lewis Phillips, UK.**
Canon 5D MkII with 24–105mm lens; f5; 1/640s; ISO 400

Brick Lane, London, UK. **Lewis Phillips, UK.**
Canon 5D MkII with 24–105mm lens; f9; 1/15s; ISO 200

Above left. While walking around the area I noticed this man waiting for the mosque to open for prayer. I asked if he would be happy to pose for an image and he agreed. I feel it represents the culture of the area well.

NEW TALENT 2013
METROPOLIS

Lewis Phillips UK
Highly Commended

Left. Another example of street artists' work. It had a big impact on me and I just had to wait until this gentleman walked past a while later to complete the picture.

Below. Street art plays a huge part in the culture of today's Brick Lane. The artist in the image is South American.

Brick Lane, London, UK. **Lewis Phillips, UK.** *Canon 5D MkII with 24–105mm lens; f5; 1/400s; ISO 400*

Craiova, Dolj county, Romania. **Felicia Simion, Romania.**
Canon 7D with 70–200mm lens; f3.5; 1/400s; ISO 100

Craiova, Dolj county, Romania. **Felicia Simion, Romania.** Canon 400D with 35–135mm lens; f4.5; 3.5s; ISO 100

Craiova, Dolj county, Romania. **Felicia Simion, Romania.** Canon 7D with 70–200mm lens; f4; 1/250s; ISO 100

NEW TALENT 2013
METROPOLIS

Felicia Simion Romania
Commended

Top left. While I was taking the photos, the little boy came and laid down on the ground, shouting up to his mother "Look Mum, an artist!"

Top right. It was a foggy Christmas morning, and I had decided to go for walk in Nicolae Romanescu Park. There was no-one around and the bridge seemed lonely, so I climbed its stairs and took this photograph.

Left. This young boy whistled for the people until the bus left the station. The frozen window and its geometry appealed to me.

FIRST SHOT 2013
EN ROUTE

This category is for less experienced amateur photographers who are still learning their craft. Stuart Draper's fascinating image is the first TPOTY category-winner to be taken on a mobile phone. As with many of the best images the appeal is not obvious but it commands a second look. It is subtle and beautifully composed. Merissa Quek's image has fantastic energy, with the moving mass of birds starkly contrasting with the stillness of the grain seller, seemingly unaware of the pandemonium surrounding him.

Sponsors of this award:

Fujifilm, Photo Iconic

Santa Teresa, Rio de Janeiro, Brazil. **Stuart Draper, UK.** *Apple iPhone 5; f2.4; 1/2300s; ISO 50*

FIRST SHOT 2013
EN ROUTE

Stuart Draper UK
Joint Winner

Previous page. As part of a local campaign to bring trams back to the region, a mural was painted in the local neighbourhood. This photo, taken from a bus window, captures a local resident on her phone, unaware that it looks as though she is waiting for the tram to arrive.

FIRST SHOT 2013
EN ROUTE

Merissa Quek Singapore
Joint Winner

Below. This grain seller, sitting by his outdoor grain store, seems unperturbed by the commotion caused by the flock of pigeons scattering just behind him.

Jaipur, India. **Merissa Quek, Singapore.** *Panasonic DMC-G1 with 45mm lens; f5.6; 1/125s; ISO100*

FIRST SHOT 2013
EN ROUTE

Matthew Coomber UK
Runner Up

This photograph was taken on the long-yet-spectacular train journey between Haputale and Kandy in Sri Lanka. My wife, Satomi, is usually the photographer; only when she wants to be in the shot herself, as in this picture, am I pressed into service!

Sri Lanka, en route from Haputale to Kandy. **Matthew Coomber, UK.** *Canon IXY Digital 220IS; f2.8; 1/100s; ISO 80*

FIRST SHOT 2013
EN ROUTE

Irina Niculicea Bulgaria
Commended

I call this image 'Symmetry of Life' because, to me, the letter M – spelled out by the lines on the water – stands for Mother since water is the cradle of life and women are associated with giving birth.

Florence, Italy. **Irina Niculicea, Bulgaria.** *Canon EOD 550D with 106mm lens; f5.6; 1/1000s; ISO 100*

BEST SINGLE IMAGE
IN A PORTFOLIO 2013

Each year there are many portfolio entries which don't win prizes but which contain outstanding individual images. In 2013 these images were chosen from the three portfolio categories - Vanishing & Emerging Cultures, Monochromal and Wild Stories - along with others which merit a special mention.

Sponsors of this award:

Genesis Imaging, Royal Geographical Society (with IBG)

Worcestershire, UK. **Pete Downing, UK.** *Canon EOS 1D MkIV with 70–200mm lens; f4; 1/3200s, ISO 1600 (auto)*

WILD STORIES

Pete Downing UK
Winner

Previous page. The kingfisher is a photographer's dream and I had spent ten hours in the hide in order to capture the moment when this azure gem broke the surface of the water and launched itself upwards towards a perch, so it might enjoy the rewards of its endeavours.

WILD STORIES

James Woodend UK
Special Mention

Below. Kirkjufell – known locally as the Wizard's Hat mountain – lit up by the Northern Lights.

Kirkjufell, Iceland. **James Woodend, UK.** *Canon 1DX with 24mm lens; f3.5; 25s; ISO 1600*

Gorner Glacier, Gornergrat, Switzerland. **Robbie Shone, UK.** *Nikon D800 with 14–24mm lens; f5; 20s; ISO 400*

WILD STORIES

Robbie Shone UK
Special Mention

Top right. Beneath the stars, two scientific explorers descend into the icy depths of the Gorner Glacier. These explorers are mapping the changes taking place as a result of global warming.

WILD STORIES

Philip Lee Harvey UK
Special Mention

Right. The Baikal–Amur Mainline (BAM) is probably the loneliest railway in the world. Started in 1974, it runs for 2,700 miles from Tayshet to Sovetskaya Gavan, across Trans-Siberia Russia.

Moscow train station, Russia. **Philip Lee Harvey, UK.** *Canon EOS 1Dx with 24–105mm lens; f7.1; 1/500s; ISO 250*

Masai Mara, Kenya. **Nicolas Lotsos, Greece.** *Nikon D300 with 70–200mm lens; f8; 1/500s; ISO 640*

WILD STORIES

Nicolas Lotsos Greece
Special Mention

Left. The night before we'd seen a pride succeed in killing a buffalo. Early the next morning, we returned to the site of the kill, but the pride was nowhere to be seen until the lioness jumped out of the tall grass, sending hyenas, jackals and vultures scattering.

WILD STORIES

Timo Palo Estonia
Special Mention

Right. My friend and I were walking on skis from the North Pole to Spitsbergen. One day, this mother and her two one-year-old cubs approached us and we had to retreat three times. On the last occasion, I decided to leave my camera on the snow shooting at intervals…

Arctic Ocean, somewhere at latitude 81 North. **Timo Palo, Estonia.**
Nikon V1 with 10mm lens; f2.8; 1/400s; ISO 100

Camargue, France. **Gail von Bergen-Ryan, Switzerland.** *Nikon D3S with 70–200mm lens; f4; 1/1000s; ISO 400*

WILD STORIES

Gail von Bergen-Ryan Switzerland
Special Mention

Above. In early morning, Camargue horses can be very quiet, standing nearly still in the water, but their strength becomes obvious when they gallop through the deep mud and water.

MONOCHROMAL

Emmanuel Coupe France
Winner

Opposite page. I have seldom witnessed waterfalls with so much raw strength as those seen across Iceland. As I walked on the path towards Gullfoss waterfall one October day, there was not a soul to be seen and the spray coming from the fall made it seem as if a rainstorm was present. Taking photographs under such challenging conditions was a great adventure.

Opposite page. Gullfoss waterfall, Iceland.
Emmanuel Coupe, France.
Canon D800E with 21mm lens; f8; 30s; ISO 200

MONOCHROMAL

Nicolas Lotsos Greece
Special Mention

A shipwreck lies in the shallow water at Salamina Passage with fog and light forming the backdrop. The history of this shipwreck remains a mystery to this day.

Salamina, Greece. **Nicolas Lotsos, Greece.**
Nikon D700 with 24–70mm lens; f16; 30s; ISO 200

MONOCHROMAL

Simon Morris UK
Special Mention

This young merchant used to make copper bangles and I spent some time trying to converse with him each day.

Rajasthan village, India. **Simon Morris, UK.**
Nikon D700 with 28–70mm lens; f5.6; 1/125s; ISO 200

MONOCHROMAL

Tony Burns UK
Special Mention

A footballer acrobatically performs a 'bicyclette' on Leblon Beach beneath the backdrop of Rio's famous Dois Irmãos ('Two Brothers') mountains.

Ipanema beach, Rio de Janeiro, Brazil. **Tony Burns, UK.**
Canon 5D MkIII with 35mm lens; f2; 1/5000s; ISO 50

Kurile Lake, Kamchatka, Russia. **Marco Urso, Italy.** *Canon EOS 1DX with 500mm lens; f6.3; 1/2000s; ISO 800*

MONOCHROMAL

Marco Urso Italy
Special Mention

Above. Russia's Kurile Lake has an abundance of Sockeye salmon that attracts plenty of brown bears. I got this shot by placing my tripod in the path of the bear and then moving away quickly after clicking!

MONOCHROMAL

Gail von Bergen-Ryan Switzerland
Special Mention

The hands and feet of a gorilla in Rwanda's Virunga Mountains. Even the young skin is tough and wrinkled, and their nails have a bizarre manicured quality.

Virunga Mountains, Rwanda. **Gail von Bergen-Ryan, Switzerland.** *Nikon D3S with 70–200mm lens; f6.7; 1/350s; ISO 1250*

MONOCHROMAL

Neil Buchan-Grant UK
Special Mention

Opposite page. This shot incorporates what I am still striving to find – and what makes one photographer stand out from another: a way of uniquely interpreting the beauty and drama we see every day.

Winchester, UK. **Neil Buchan-Grant, UK.** *Olympus OMD-EM5 with 12mm lens; f5; 1/500s; ISO 200*

VANISHING AND EMERGING CULTURES

Roberto Nistri Italy
Winner

I spent two weeks along the sandy banks of the Ganges in Allahabad, in order to document Maha Kumbh Mela – the largest religious festival on the planet. Approximately 100 million pilgrims gather in this sacred city between the end of January and the first days of March. In order to take this picture I had to get into the cold waters of the Ganges, and wait for the spectacular collective dive of the Naga Sadhus – naked holy men who spend most of their lives in meditation amid the mountains, deserts and forests of India.

Allahabad, India. **Roberto Nistri, Italy.** *Nikon D700 with 70–200mm lens; f5.6; 1/500s; ISO 500*

Kibish, Ethiopia. **Toby Adamson, UK.** *Canon 5D MkIII, with 70mm lens; f5.6; 1/125s; ISO 100*

Nevada, USA. **Peter Gordon, Ireland.** *Nikon D3X with 24–70mm lens; f2.8; 1/160s; ISO 1600*

Guizhou, China. **Kieron Nelson, Canada.**
Nikon D3 with 24–70mm lens; f4; 1/125s; ISO 200

VANISHING AND EMERGING CULTURES

Peter Gordon Ireland
Special Mention

Above right. Every year a temple is built at the Burning Man Festival in the Nevada Desert. It provides a space for visitors to discuss life and death and at the end of the event the temple is burned so the catharsis is complete.

VANISHING AND EMERGING CULTURES

Toby Adamson UK
Special Mention

Above left. A young Suri man from the tiny village of Kibish in southwestern Ethiopia. The Suri are semi-nomadic cattle herders who take great pride in their appearance – body adornments like the necklace shown above are common. Sadly, their identity and traditional customs are under threat due to government intervention and development in the region.

VANISHING AND EMERGING CULTURES

Kieron Nelson Canada
Special Mention

Left. During holidays and festivals, Changjiao Miao women shape their hair into massive decorative buns using linen, wool, and small amounts of ancestral hair. These buns can weigh up to two kilograms.

VANISHING AND EMERGING CULTURES

Tariq Sawyer Switzerland
Special Mention

Right. A Kazakh-Mongolian nomad leads his herd of sheep out into a near whiteout in search of grazing grounds, which have been cut off due to sub-zero temperatures and heavy snowfall.

Altai Mountains. Bayan-Ulgii Aimag, Mongolia. **Tariq Sawyer, Switzerland.**
Canon 5D MkIII with 16–35mm lens; f4; 1/8000s; ISO 200

VANISHING AND EMERGING CULTURES

Sahil Lodha India
Special Mention

Opposite page. This photograph attempts to capture the energy and passion with which people celebrate Holi, the festival of colours. As a kid, I loved it because I was allowed to go absolutely insane: throwing water balloons and splashing colour everywhere.

VANISHING AND EMERGING CULTURES

Simon Morris UK
Special Mention

Left. This boy, Jack, lived with his family on the Malecón in a small apartment that had once been grand, but was now dilapidated. Yet there was still beauty amid the ruin.

Havana, Cuba. **Simon Morris, UK.**
Leica M9 with 35mm lens; f2.8; 1/30s; ISO 500

Mathura, Uttar Pradesh, India. **Sahil Lodha, India.** *Canon 50D with 18–55mm lens; f11; 1/200s; ISO 100*

10 for 10

Tim Bird UK. Overall Winner

In 2013, as part of TPOTY's 10th anniversary celebration, we ran a monthly single image competition, 10 for 10, where blog visitors could vote for their favourite image. Then, once we had the 10 winning shots, our judges assessed them and chose the overall winner. This is that winning image.

Udaipur, India. **Tim Bird, UK.** *Fujifilm X-Pro1 with 18-55mm lens; f16; 8s; ISO 400*

JUDGES

The TPOTY judging panel is international and made up of experts from the world of photography and travel. They are selected to reflect a variety of backgrounds, styles and attitudes to photography and the photographic image. A key element of the panel is the wealth of visual and specialist expertise brought into the mix by our technical and creative judges. Lay judges and past winners have also participated, bringing fresh views and perspectives to the judging process.

These judges give their time because they are passionate about photography, and we are immensely grateful for their efforts.

We would like to thank the 2013 judging panel:

Judges

Steve Bloom - travel & wildlife photographer

Chris Coe - photographer, author & lecturer

Colin Finlay - stock photography expert

Jeremy Hoare - photographer & TV cameraman

Debbie Ireland - picture editor & curator

Eamonn McCabe - award-winning photographer & picture editor

Nick Meers - landscape & panoramic photographer

Caroline Metcalfe - director of photography, Condé Nast Traveller

Mary Robert - head of photography, Richmond, the American International University in London

Emma Thomson - award-winning travel writer & editor

Chris Weston - wildlife photographer

Manfred Zollner - photographic critic and deputy editor in chief, Fotomagazin

SPONSORS AND PARTNERS

Cutty Sark

Cutty Sark blended Scotch is an iconic whisky; its distinctive yellow label has graced the world's best bars and clubs for nearly 90 years. The first light-coloured blended whisky, it was launched at the height of cocktail culture in the 1920s and it has remained synonymous with enjoying great drinks in great company ever since. The brand keeps cropping up in popular culture, a constant reminder of the status of the brand. It is always the choice of adventurous characters! Cutty Sark's major markets are now Spain, Greece, Portugal, and the USA.
www.cutty-sark.com

Harley-Davidson®

Warr's was founded on the Kings Road, London (England) in 1924 by Captain Frederick James Warr, becoming an official Harley-Davidson® dealer that same year. In 1949 F.J's son Fred Warr left the Royal Air Force and went to work for his father. Although post-War business was very tough, by the 1960's Fred Jnr had become Britain's Harley-Davidson® distributor. In 1999 the company moved into a new purpose-built 20,000 sq ft dealership built on the site of the original 1920s' store. In 2003 a further Harley dealership was opened in Mottingham, South London. From those early days up to today, Warr's has been synonymous with Harley-Davidson® and is Europe's oldest and certainly most successful Harley-Davidson® dealership Group. Today Warr's dealerships are still owned and operated by the Warr family and form a part of the Warr Group of companies.
www.warrs.com

railbookers

Railbookers

Railbookers is an independent travel company, specialising in tailor made rail holidays across Europe and the world. Established in 2003, Railbookers have offices in London, Sydney, Los Angeles and Auckland. We aim to deliver exceptional travel experiences by rail as we believe the journey is part of the holiday. Customers have the opportunity to put together their own tailor made holiday with expert guidance. They have the complete freedom to choose what they want to do and when they want to do it, safe in the knowledge that everything has been expertly arranged and that we are only a phone call away.
www.railbookers.com

always extraordinary | cazenove+loyd

cazenove+loyd

cazenove+loyd are the experts in experiential travel. Started over 20 years ago by Henrietta Loyd, they create tailor-made trips to three exciting and challenging parts of the world, Africa + Indian Ocean, South + South East Asia and Central + South America. They also design a selection of intimate and exclusive small group experiences that offer unprecedented private access to some of the world's most inspiring places and cultures. Extraordinary experiences for every client.
www.cazloyd.com

Plastic Sandwich

Plastic Sandwich has been putting together portfolios for photographers and art directors since the early 1970s. It was founded, and is still run, by Joyce Pinto and Rob Jacobs - who has been with the company for over 30 years. Between them they have unparalleled experience in the field of image presentation in its various forms over the last 40 years and have been the proud sponsors of the TPOTY competition since 2003. Plastic Sandwich's services are also utilised by companies such as event and PR organisations, film companies, high-end presenters, and anyone whose activities or craft are best shown through the presentation of images. We are now direct suppliers to Jaguar Land Rover.
www.plasticsandwich.co.uk

Yosemite/Mariposa Co. Tourism Bureau

Just three hours from San Francisco, Yosemite National Park beholds four seasons of splendor. Take in the wonders of one of America's greatest national treasures with a guided naturalist hike, photography class, snowshoe trek or a high country walk. Enhance your visit with a mountain bike ride, a walk in the footsteps of John Muir, glide on a zip line, enjoy a real Wild West bar in Coulterville, explore the authentic gold rush era town of Mariposa, sip local wine and craft beer, dine on local food, or take in a unique regional event.
www.yosemiteexperience.com

Opposite page. Southern Iceland. **Emmanuel Coupe, France.**
Nikon D800E with 24-70mm lens; f9; 1/3200s; ISO 200

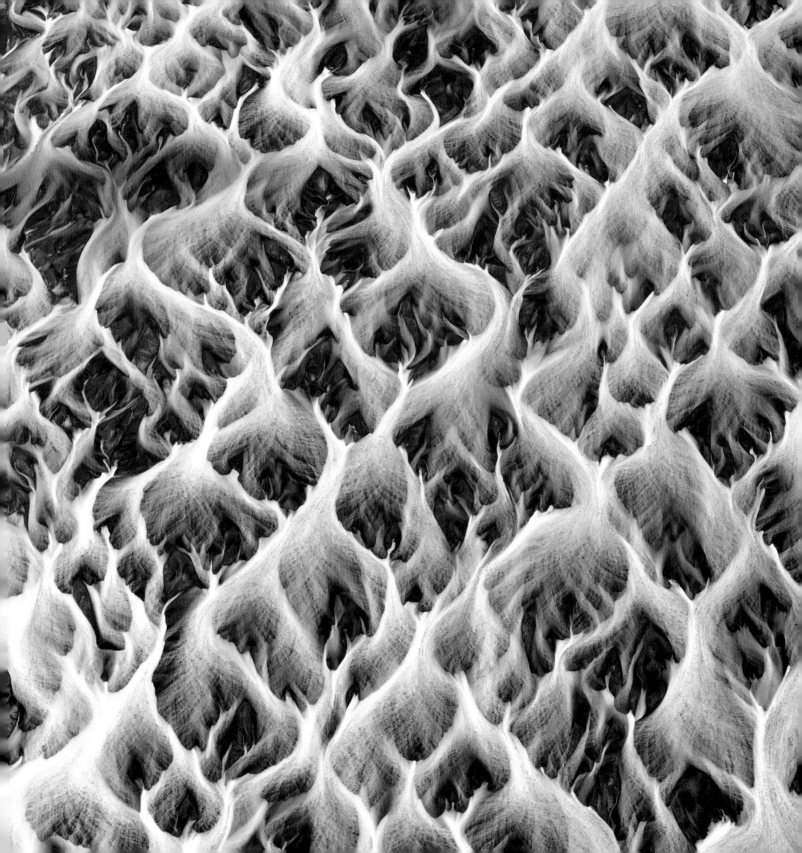

SPONSORS AND PARTNERS

Genesis Imaging

One of the UK's leading photographic image printers, Genesis Imaging is in the unique position of offering all manner of photographic printing, mounting and framing services for the creative industry. They believe photographic printing is an art. They print images of the highest calibre for some of the best-known professional photographers, artists and art galleries around – people who demand the very best quality available. Their superb Giclée Fine Art and Lambda prints have graced the walls of numerous famous galleries, from London's National Portrait Gallery to New York's Museum of Modern Art. Genesis Imaging print and mount all the Travel Photographer of the Year exhibitions.

www.genesisimaging.co.uk

Connekt Colour

Founded in 1991, Connekt Colour has 20 years of colour and colour reproduction experience. Their impressive portfolio of longstanding clients is testimony to their consistent levels of quality and service. They view themselves very much as an extension of you and your clients' business and are always keen to be involved from the start of a project, offering advice and solutions to get a better job or save you money. In 2009 they were awarded Best Digital Book of The Year at the British Book Design and Production Awards and in 2010 their digital partner, Litho Division, won Best Photographic Art/Architecture Monograph Book. Connekt Colour prints all the Travel Photographer of the Year portfolio books and cards.

www.connektcolour.com

FUJIFILM

Fujifilm

Fujifilm is a global leader in imaging technology, products and services including digital cameras, photofinishing, digital storage and recording media, consumer and professional film, motion picture film, professional video, printing systems, medical imaging, office technology, flat panel displays and graphic arts. The company employs more than 73,000 people worldwide, with 178 subsidiaries stretching across four continents. In the UK, Fujifilm has been supplying the imaging, printing and graphics industries, as well as consumers, professional and enthusiast photographers, with high quality, innovative products and services for over 25 years. All the TPOTY exhibition prints are produced on Fujifilm Crystal Archive paper and Direct to Media.

www.fujifilm.eu/uk

Direct Photographic

With offices in London, Paris and Cape Town, Direct Photographic is dedicated to delivering the very best in rental equipment to photographers Worldwide. An active supporter of the industry as a whole, Direct Photographic is a keen investor in the latest equipment and remains committed to helping capture the vision of both emerging and established photographers. With an extensive range of products, including the latest in HD camera and LED lighting technology, plus continual investment throughout every aspect of its business, Direct Photographic is the perfect choice for every photographic project. Direct Photographic light the Travel Photographer of the Year exhibition at the Royal Geographical Society (with IBG) in London.

www.directphotographic.co.uk

iriðius

Iridius

Iridius offers a wide range of design and training services to a growing list of clients, including Adobe, Hewlett Packard, Royal Doulton, Porsche, Audi, Transco, Warner Lambert, Top Yachts, MEM Consumer Finance, Harper Collins, Streamline, Faversham House Group, Travel Photographer of the Year and numerous small to medium enterprises. Although they are a small team, they use this to their advantage: they don't have administration and management overheads and they work quickly and efficiently. Iridius design the Travel Photographer of the Year "Journey" portfolio books and website.

www.iridius.co.uk

photo iconic

Photo Iconic

Photo Iconic offers a range of TPOTY photography courses, workshops and masterclasses to suit all abilities and styles of photography, all tutored by award-winning photographers. These range from half-day workshops to one-week courses and include the festival of photography - Travel Photography Live - in association with Travel Photographer of the Year (TPOTY). Photo Iconic also runs the TPOTY Photo Tours; a selection of photographic holidays and adventures to some of the world's most interesting and inspiring destinations.

www.photoiconic.com.

SPONSORS AND PARTNERS

Royal Geographical Society (with IBG)

The Royal Geographical Society (with The Institute of British Geographers) was formed in 1830 for 'the advancement of geographical science'. Today, they deliver this objective by developing, supporting and promoting geography through research, expeditions and fieldwork, education, and public engagement, while also providing geographical input to policy. They hold the world's largest private geographical collection and provide public access to it. In 2011 the Society embarked on a five-year partnership with Travel Photographer of the Year to host major annual exhibitions of the awards' stunning travel photography, supported by an ongoing programme of workshops and events.

www.rgs.org

Lesser Flamingos, Ndutu Lake, Ngorongoro conservation area, Tanzania.
André Gilden, Netherlands. *Nikon D3S with 500mm lens; f4.5; 1/640s; ISO 2000*

61 year-old Rahjan, Andaman Islands. **Valerie Leonard, France.** *Nikon D3S with 24mm lens; f13; 1/160s; ISO 400*

INDEX OF PHOTOGRAPHERS

We would like to thank the photographers whose images appear in this book. Their support, along with that of all the other photographers from across the world who enter the awards, makes the Travel Photographer of the Year awards and this book possible.

Adamson, Toby	85	**Lotsos,** Nicolas	57, 78, 81
Allen, Timothy	7, 8, 9, 10, 11	**Morris,** Simon	26, 27, 81, 86
Baeck, Gerald	58	**Mott,** Justin	53, Back cover
Bird, Tim	88	**Nelson,** Kieron	85
Buchan-Grant, Neil	83	**Ng,** Kokkai	61
Burns, Tony	81, Back cover	**Niculicea,** Irina	73
Conning, Judith	61	**Nistri,** Roberto	39, 84
Coomber, Matthew	73	**Oliete,** David	Frontispiece, 56
Coupe, Emmanuel	36, 37, 80, 91	**Palo,** Timo	78
Dall'Angelo, Barbara	48, 49	**Pepper,** Tom	63, 64, 65
Deckmyn, Myriam	21	**Phillips,** Lewis	68
Doest, Jasper	41, 42, 43, Back cover	**Pisati,** Beniamino	38
Downing, Pete	75	**Prasasya,** Patria	18, 19
Draper, Stuart	71	**Quek,** Merissa	72
Edwards, Jason	28, 29, 55	**Rystrøm,** Jonathan	13, 14, 15
Gilden, André	93	**Salak,** Jovian	20
Gordon, Peter	85	**Sawyer,** Tariq	86
Gough, Gavin	23, 24, 25	**Shone,** Robbie	77
Guttman, Chase	16, 17	**Simion,** Felicia	69
Haglund, Johnny	44, 45, 96	**Singh,** Satpal	51
Harvey, Philip Lee	77	**Steeley,** Terry	4
Hetherington, Ed	46, 47	**Tan,** Sheng Hong	66, 67
Johanson, Jørgen	5	**Taylor,** Tim	50, 54
Lazar, David	31, 59	**Urso,** Marco	3, 60, 82
Lee, Jino	Front cover, 33, 34, 35	**Vinton,** Cat	30
Leonard, Valerie	94	**von Bergen-Ryan,** Gail	79, 82
Lodha, Sahil	87, Back cover	**Woodend,** James	76

Salt worker and camels, Lake Asele, Ethiopia. **Johnny Haglund, Norway.** *Canon EOS 1DS MkIII with 24-70mm lens; f20; 1/125s; ISO 320*

TAKE ANOTHER JOURNEY, JOIN US ON ANOTHER ADVENTURE.

Journey One
2003-04

Journey Two
2005-06

Journey Three
2007-08

Journey Four
2010-11

Journey Five
2012

Visit www.tpoty.com to buy Journeys One to Five, or enter Travel Photographer of the Year
for a chance to see your photography published in a future Journey portfolio.